CONTENTS

Table of Contents

ACRONYMS

AUC	Association of Ukrainian Cities
EU	European Union
CIDA	Canadian International Development Agency
CoU	Constitution of Ukraine
GIZ	German Society for International Cooperation
GOU	Government of Ukraine
SDC	Swiss Agency for Development and Cooperation
SIDA	Sweden International Development Cooperation Agency
UNDP	United Nations Development Programme
USAID	United States Agency for International Development
USG	United States Government

EXECUTIVE SUMMARY

This report is the result of an extensive assessment of the process of proposed decentralization reforms in Ukraine as it relates to the future programming of USAID/Ukraine. Fieldwork for the assessment took place during most of the month of July 2014 and included over 50 semi-structured interviews with key stakeholders in seven cities in addition to seven citizen focus groups conducted in four different cities. The three primary questions that the assessment sought to address are: 1) what is the current operating environment for local governance reforms?; 2) what is the capacity and capacity-building needs of local governments and civil society to implement such reforms and effectively exercise improved governance on the local level?; and 3) what are the existing and planned donor efforts in local governance and decentralization?

With regards to the first question, the assessment team found that there exist mixed prospects for decentralization reform. On the one hand, there is widespread public support and political will within the present government for the reform, and many stakeholders view its implementation as an urgent priority to move Ukraine towards integration with the European community. On the other hand, vested interests in the present system related to the entrenched patron-client nature of politics in Ukraine threaten to undermine the prospects of meaningful decentralization that may cut-off existing avenues for rent-seeking on the national-level. Additionally, while there appears to be political will at high levels of governance, including President Poroshenko, many experts and political actors have yet to accept the present formulation of the reform more due to issues related to political competition at the national level than to the reform's role in empowering local governments. In particular, many of the national-level political actors are wary that decentralization reform proposed by the presidency will serve to strengthen the president vis-à-vis the parliament and cabinet of ministers. As a result, most of the parties in parliament did not support the version of the reform presented by the presidency over the summer. At present, the implementation of reform has been delayed at least until a new parliament can be elected in late October 2014. These elections could either provide a better or worse environment for adopting legislation needed for the decentralization reform depending upon the configuration of political forces it creates.

In general, it is likely that the realization of reforms will require negotiation on various points in the proposed plan for decentralization. In addition to the question of whether national oversight of local governments will be performed by the presidency, the cabinet of ministers, or a combination of Ukraine's dual executive power structure, another controversial question that will likely need to be negotiated relates to the consolidations of villages (*hromada*) and *rayons*.[1] Proposals suggest shrinking the number of *hromada* from about 15,000 to 1,200 and the number of *rayons* from about 500 to 100. This would make the proposed empowerment of *hromadas* in the country much more feasible, ensuring that each had the minimal human capital and technical capacity to implement self-governance. Additionally, this reform would make efforts to support each local government more feasible for the *oblast* and national level governments (as well as for international donors). However, many on the local level express concern that the proposal to consolidate *hromada* and *rayons* would adversely impact their existing access to health care clinics and schools. Furthermore, this reform is also likely to face opposition from many local interest groups, who would potentially lose their positions of power within the present configuration of territorial-administrative units. It is particularly pertinent that such opposition to territorial administrative consolidation derailed attempts

---

[1] The term *hromada* has a variety of interpretations in the Ukrainian language, which has created some confusion regarding its use in decentralization plans as the primary territorial unit of governance, roughly equal to a village. For example, *hromada* also means "community" in Ukrainian, which is an ambiguous term that encompasses informal communities, groups of citizens, and the formal unit of "village." In this report, the authors use the term to refer to the most local unit of governance proposed in decentralization reform plans.

at decentralization reform in 2006-08. As a result, it is very possible that the present reform effort could end up being carried out without this important consolidation of territorial units. If such a scenario were to happen, the reforms would result in much less change in the nature of governance, and they would likely only really impact larger territorial units, such as "district towns" and potentially *rayons*. *Hromadas*, which are envisioned as the central unit of governance, would not be able to take over their envisioned expanded responsibilities if they remain the small population centers they are today.

Finally, the conflict that continues in eastern Ukraine creates further complications for the decentralization process. At present, the national government does not control key areas of Donetsk and Luhansk oblasts, and it is unclear if and when these regions will return to the control of the Ukrainian state. Although the decentralization reforms can serve as critical means for re-integrating these regions into the state on the terms of the local population, there remains a serious threat that portions of eastern Ukraine will either fully secede from Ukraine or become disputed regions not beholden at all to Kyiv as has occurred in Georgia with Ossetia and Abkhazia or in Moldova with Transnistria. If this occurs, it will be virtually impossible to implement the proposed decentralization reforms in these eastern territories. How this particular situation is resolved will obviously also depend upon Russia and its intentions in supporting separatists in eastern Ukraine. Even if prospects improve for re-integrating these regions into a unified Ukrainian state, the reform will need to carefully balance allowing these regions substantial latitude for self-governance with the necessity to have them follow the constitution and national laws of Ukraine.

With regards to the second question, the assessment team found that both local government and local civil society capacity varied by the nature of the territorial-administrative units in question. In "regional cities," the capacity of both government officials and civil society is quite adequate. While these actors would need some capacity-building to adjust to changing authorities within the country's governance structure, their present level of sophistication is already quite high. The capacity on the *rayon* and *hromada* level, however, is presently very low. Especially if the reform proceeds in its present form and *hromada* become the primary units of governance on the local level, there will be a very large need for capacity-building work with both *hromada* councils and local civil society. Of course, it is more feasible for the international community to assist with this capacity-building if the present 15,000 *hromada* are consolidated into 1,200 larger units. Across all levels of government, there will be a need for training in new financial systems intended to provide increased resources to the local level. In *hromada* and *rayons*, there will be a need for assistance to local councils on procedures, engaging citizens, forming budgets (ideally in a participatory way), and doing strategic planning. Local civil society, at least on the regional level, needs assistance with the professionalization of their "watchdog" activities to ensure that newly empowered local governments have substantive and effective citizen oversight. Likewise, there is a need to cultivate local analytical centers, which can help inform government policy and strategic planning.

At present, most donors involved in decentralization are focused on assisting the reform process by supporting various local experts, who are in turn helping to inform government reform plans, and various donors have smaller pilot projects around the country that assist local governments, community organizations, and NGOs. Additionally, there are various regional funds available via the European Union for local Ukrainian municipalities to support new initiatives that can help bolster the decentralization process. Most donors with whom the assessment team spoke stressed the need for more "on-the-ground" work in local municipalities, *rayons*, and *hromada*. It was also evident that the international community has yet to provide much assistance on the financial mechanisms for decentralization, perhaps waiting until the political issues related to the reform are ironed out. Finally, some donors are providing assistance to the GOU with public education on decentralization reforms, but our focus groups found that these efforts have yet to reach most people in the country, who remain generally ignorant of the reforms' proposed details.

I. BACKGROUND ON ASSESSMENT

Purpose of Assessment

Over the last several months, Ukraine has undergone monumental changes, including the election of a new president and establishment of a new government that are dedicated to democratic reforms and to the integration of the country into the European community. Amidst these changes, the USAID Mission in Ukraine believes that there are strong indications that the government and president wish to implement needed decentralization reforms that can empower local authorities and ensure that they have the resources to exercise broader responsibilities. As a result, the Mission requested that an assessment team examine the efforts being undertaken by the presidency, government, and parliament to implement decentralization reforms. Sean R. Roberts, Director of the International Development Studies program at The George Washington University, led the assessment team tackling this task, and Oleksandr Fisun, Chair of the Political Science Department at Kharkiv National University, joined him as the team's local expert. Faye Haselkorn of USAID's Europe and Eurasia Bureau in Washington, DC also joined the team for part of the assessment and was instrumental in particular in gathering information regarding the involvement of other donors in Ukraine's decentralization reforms. Finally, Olga Prokhorchuk supported the logistics for the assessment and assisted with recommendations for civil society organizations with whom to meet, Victor Rachkevych, Kira (Mickie) Mitre, and Veeraya (Kate) Somvongsiri of USAID/Ukraine were instrumental in providing technical guidance, and Yana Zhambekova was indispensible in helping to obtain meetings with important national-level government officials.

In particular, the USAID Mission outlined three central questions to be answered by the assessment team: 1) what is the current operating environment for local governance reforms?; 2) what is the capacity and capacity-building needs of local governments to implement such reforms and effectively exercise increased authority?; and 3) what are the existing and planned donor efforts in local governance and decentralization? The assessment team added to the second research question an analysis of the capacities and needs of local civil society in implementing such reforms successfully since it is anticipated that any successful decentralization reform will require strong civil society involvement in oversight of local governance. In addition to answering these questions, the assessment team was tasked with providing recommendations to the mission regarding future programming priorities related to decentralization and local governance development.

Historical Background of Decentralization Reform in Ukraine

In order to understand the reasons that USAID and other international actors anticipate that Ukraine will implement decentralization reforms in the near future, it is important to understand the history of decentralization and local governance reforms in the country since independence. While the scope of this assessment does not warrant an in-depth analysis and recounting of this history, a brief summary of the critical events relating to decentralization in Ukraine and their progression is appropriate.

Ukraine has struggled with democratic reforms since the country's independence was declared in 1991. Although formally the country has the legislation in place to implement most aspects of democratization, implementation of this legislation has long been very uneven due to corruption and informal power structures in the country. Rights to local self-governance encompassing significant elements of state decentralization have long been guaranteed in the country, beginning with the 1996 constitution and the 1997 "Law on Local Self-Governance in Ukraine." However, most of these rights have not been fully exercised, and the central government has generally sought to control local affairs of the state to differing degrees dependent upon the administration in power. Many experts with whom the assessment team met, for example, suggested that local governmental bodies were most empowered in the late 1990s under President Leonid Kuchma after the passing of the 1997 law on local self-governance, but subsequently Kuchma began centralizing state powers, at least de-facto, in the early 2000s.

While Kuchma's presidency became increasingly embroiled in corruption scandals in the early 2000s, he did agree to step-down from power in compliance with the constitution and did not run in the 2004 presidential elections. However, he did back a candidate in that election, Viktor Yanukovych, who had served as Governor of Donetsk Oblast from 1997 to 2002 and as Kuchma's Prime Minister from 2002-2004. In addition to being viewed as Kuchma's hand-picked successor, Yanukovych was considered pro-Russian at a time when many Ukrainians were seeking to limit ties with their northern neighbor and strengthen ties with the European Union. Representing the country's pro-European constituency, Viktor Yushchenko ran against Yanukovych in a tightly contested and controversial second-round election in November 2004. Although Yanukovych was initially declared the winner of the election, large protests claiming electoral fraud eventually forced a re-vote in which Yushchenko was declared the winner in January of 2005. After the controversial second round of elections that spurred large popular protests, the parliament also approved a new constitution that sought to limit the power of the president and strengthen that of the parliament, which was now given the power of ratifying presidential appointments to the position of Prime Minister, who subsequently was empowered to form the government.

Yushchenko had an ambitious plan for democratic reforms that involved bringing the country closer to European standards of democratic governance, but he had few substantive successes partly due to his difficult relationships with subsequent Prime Ministers. One of the reforms that he pursued was a reinforcement of the decentralization of the state, an effort largely spearheaded by then Deputy Prime Minister Roman Bezsmertnyi.[2] In 2008, Yushchenko sought to establish a new constitution, which included, among other things, increased authority and independence for local units of government as well as a consolidation of territorial units that would reduce the size of government and ensure more uniformity in the size of population governed by any given unit of local self-governance. These constitutional changes were never realized, and there was very little progress in decentralization during Yushchenko's presidency. Overall, many in Ukraine were disappointed with Yushchenko's presidency, which had generally been unable to deliver on the democratic reforms and progress with European integration it had initially promised.

In 2010, Yushchenko overwhelmingly lost his bid for re-election, not even passing to the second round. In the second round, Viktor Yanukovych, whom Yuschhenko had defeated five years earlier, defeated Yulia Tymoschenko. Although Yanukovych had formerly been viewed as favoring ties with Russia over those with the EU, during his first years as president, he appeared to be balancing relations with both Russia and the EU. While careful to retain positive relations with Russia, he continued to pursue ties with Europe and signed an agreement with the EU on an "action plan" that was to further the process of Ukraine's European integration. In terms of democratization and decentralization, Yanukovych's presidency was generally viewed as moving backwards. His administration pushed to abolish the 2004 constitutional amendments, and he did much to re-centralize power in the central government and in the presidency in particular. His government also found grounds to arrest his primary political opponent, Yulia Tymoshenko, as well as other prominent opposition figures, effectively weakening any opposition to his rule. His political party, *The Party of Regions*, operated as a political machine throughout the country, and those local government administrations it controlled tended to implement policies directed from the center. Likewise, much evidence exists that those local administrations controlled by other parties suffered

---

[2] See http://www.president.gov.ua/en/news/7536.html

under his presidency by receiving less resources from the central government. His administration also succeeded in rolling back local control over numerous governmental decisions, including the lucrative field of land allocation and new construction projects, which were now decided on the level of the central government rather than locally.

Interestingly, Yanukovych's downfall was less due to his relatively authoritarian and centralized approaches to governance than to his about-face in foreign policy. After having entered into discussions with the EU on an Association Agreement that would have substantially furthered the European integration of Ukraine, he suddenly turned down this agreement in favor of an economic pact with Russia in November 2013. This set into motion a series of large public protests against the president around the country (known as the "EuroMaidan"), where Yanukovych's opponents also strongly criticized the corrupt nature of his administration. After Yanukovych instituted anti-protest laws and used force against the protestors during the first two months of 2014, the parliament voted to remove him from office. While he continues to suggest that he is the legitimate president of the country, he has since fled to Russia. In the aftermath of his removal, a conflict has escalated between Russia and Ukraine, first resulting in the Russian annexation of the Crimea region of Ukraine and then in Russia's sustained support for a separatist movement in the east of the country.

This situation has left the country in turmoil, but the conflict with Russia has also created strong patriotic feelings and a renewed urgency to adopt reforms that will lead to Ukraine's integration into Europe. A presidential election in May of 2014 resulted in the election of Petro Poroshenko with 54.7% of the vote, the parliament has ratified a new Prime Minister who has subsequently formed a new government, and a parliamentary vote reinstated the 2004 constitutional amendments, which had previously been removed under Yanukovych.[3] Additionally, under its new government, Ukraine has now signed the controversial EU Association Agreement that had led to Yanukovych's removal. Poroshenko has stated that decentralization is a top priority for him, and the Ministry for Regional Development led by former mayor Volodymyr Groisman is supporting the call for reform, which is also a major stipulation in the EU Association Agreement. While this process has been understandably slowed down by the country's armed conflict in the east, most supporters of the reform suggest that it is critical that the country be ready to implement decentralization reforms before the October 2015 local elections. Many of the same experts who had worked on Yushchenko and Bezsmertnyi's failed decentralization reforms previously are working with the government on new constitutional amendments now, and they are adopting a model largely based on the experience of neighboring Poland.

At the same time, many international and local experts have suggested that decentralization is the most critical reform for Ukraine at the moment. As will be further discussed below, a well designed decentralization plan could help to dismantle the vertical power structures that have been the primary forms of political power since independence, hence improving efficiency of governance and reducing at least the largest scale corruption that has continually plagued the country, especially under Viktor Yanukovych's leadership. Furthermore, decentralization that encourages local variance and is based in locally driven initiatives will be critical politically in re-uniting Ukraine in the aftermath of the divisive conflict that continues in the east of the country.

For all of these reasons, many of the local experts with whom the assessment team met suggested that serious progress on decentralization reforms is critical to Ukraine's future and must be adopted as quickly as possible. The most passionate stakeholders even suggested that a failure of this reform could lead to the failure of the Ukrainian state all together given the other pressures the country presently faces. At the same time, most local experts acknowledged that this reform would not be easy either politically or technically. The challenges faced by the reforms and the important role they

---

[3] Arseniy Yatsenuk was appointed Prime Minister in the aftermath of Yanukovych's removal from power, and his position was ratified by the parliament. During the assessment, Yatsenuk submitted his resignation from the post, but the parliament declined his resignation.

can play in democratizing Ukraine's present model of governance are discussed below in the analysis of the country's general political economy.

Political Economy Analysis: Challenges and Promises of Decentralization

More generally, the Ukrainian political regime to date has been characterized by the competition between different patron-client groups over political/economic institutions, which can provide opportunities for rent extraction. This regime type is notable for its lack of effective and rational bureaucracy and the absence of institutional separation between economic and political spheres. While these features have been central to the process of modern state formation in Ukraine, they also lessen the strength of formal institutions in favor of informal means of asserting power. Additionally, they undermine the concept of meritocracy both in political and economic spheres in favor of a system based on personal connections as client-patron groups serve as the primary vehicle to obtain political influence and wealth through both the capture of state/public institutions and the extraction of resources. These principals have made it difficult for even reformist politicians dedicated to democratization, such as former president Victor Yuschenko, to make meaningful changes to governance that positively impact the daily lives of citizens. In looking at the prospects for decentralization reforms, it is critical to understand these informal aspects of power in Ukraine and the constraints they potentially place on the success of the reforms.

As a result of these informal aspects of power in the country, Ukraine has historically been a state where power is strongly concentrated in the presidency despite numerous attempts to create a formal balance of powers in governmental structure. In the absence of effective and non-biased private property protection and amidst competition between various political/economic groups, major players seeking economic and political power in the country work to become associated with the patron-client network of the president, who concentrates formal and informal powers. Political scientists in the United States have come to characterize this system as a "Patronal Presidential" form of governance. The alliance between the President and major political/economical players is a zero-sum game, because it relies on the concentration of power in the presidency and his/her close associates at the explicit expense of other major players. On the one hand, this system greatly strengthens the power of the president, who can re-distribute resources, suppress dissent and transfer externalities to alternative political/economic players in an effective way. On the other hand, under a patronal presidency, the head of state becomes dependent on influential political/economic actors, often referred to as "oligarchs," effectively concentrating power in a corporate group of loyalists, cronies and supporters rather than in the exclusive hands of an all-powerful president who is as dependent upon this group as they are on him or her. Ukrainian experts call this corporate group "the Family," which consists of cronies, relatives, and other loyal supporters, and it can limit the ability of even the most reform-minded president to tackle real structural reform of the political system.

If this system works on the principal of concentrated power, it is far from immune from opposition. In fact, the political history of Ukraine can be portrayed as the rise and fall of a series of "patronal presidencies." As one "Family" of power becomes stronger, it inevitably disrupts the inter-elite consensus in the country and drives some major players to join the opposition and utilize their influence to weaken the power of the president and his circle. This has led to two major regime changes in the last decade, when presidents have been forcibly removed by public protest movements backed by figures from the oligarchy rather than waiting for leadership changes facilitated through the political process. In this sense, one can characterize the Ukrainian political process since the late 1990s as cyclical with alternating movements to strengthen and weaken the power of the "patronal presidency." For example, under Kuchma between 1999 and 2004, there was an attempt to strengthen presidential powers, which led to the "Orange Revolution" of 2004/2005 and a five-year period of an attempted weakening of the presidency. This was followed by a reassertion of presidential power between 2010 and 2014 under Yanukovych, which led to the backlash of the "EuroMaidan" protests that unseated him and are now ushering in a new period of weakening presidential power.

In this context, the major questions regarding proposed decentralization reforms is whether they can break this unstable cycle of governance that alternates between strong and weak centralized presidential power and whether they can supplant the existing vertical power structures that facilitate this system, both the formal one of the state and the informal ones of powerful interest groups, with a power structure that is more horizontal and localized. The powerful role of major political/economic players, or "oligarchs," in this cycle problematizes both of these questions. If one examines the most recent manifestation of the cycle, beginning with the reassertion of central presidential power under Yanukovych and ending with his removal from power, it becomes obvious that major interest groups have played a critical role in the overthrow of Yanukovych and correspondingly could now seek to exert their interests at the expense of those of others in a post-Yanukovych environment. Hence, while proposed post-EuroMaidan reforms appear to be aimed at weakening presidential powers, there is a real threat that some interest groups who sought to unseat Yanukovych may seek to reassert presidential powers through a new "Family," regardless of the wishes of the president himself.

After the 2010 presidential elections, Yanukovych began reasserting the "patronal presidency" model with the assistance of a "Family" of powerful political/economic players (i.e. Oleksandr Yanukovych, Serhiy Arbuzov, Vitaliy Zaharchenko, Oleksandr Klymenko, Serhiy Kurchenko) and using the structure of a strong political party, the Party of Regions, which was based in centralized decision-making and loyalty. By 2012, Viktor Yanukovych had substantially consolidated his position, entrenching the system of the "patronal presidency." However, relying exclusively on the power of these two structures – the "Family" and the Party of Regions, Yanukovych also began directly challenging the power of other important interest groups in the country. This transpired through the re-distribution of assets and resources in the favor of those powerful interest groups that supported Yanukovych's regime since there were few new resources to be appropriated or "privatized" as had been the case previously. For example, the assertion of the interest of Yanukovych in the hydrocarbon market and the dispute over *Aerosvit* airlines led to a direct conflict with Ihor Kolomoiskyi. In addition, Yanukovych provoked antagonism from other interest groups by transferring Oleksandr Yaroslavsky's property to Serhiy Kurchenko.

This re-distribution of resources to Yanukovych's "Family" also affected economic players beyond the major economic actors in the country, including the middle class and the wider population, through extensive "top-down" rent-seeking activities that manifested themselves locally as daily corruption. As a result, a broad coalition developed around the "EuroMaidan" protests that toppled the incumbent regime and began deconstructing Yanukovych's "patronal presidency." However, one cannot deny that oligarchic forces played a central role in driving the overthrow of Yanukovych, and these forces could now seek means to exert their political and economic power more effectively, thus potentially undermining further democratization, decentralization, and transparency. While the post-EuroMaidan leadership in Ukraine is clearly dedicated to democratic reform and European integration, the powerful legacy of informal political and economic institutions in the country will make the realization of these goals difficult as various interest groups may seek to assert their interests over and through the office of the presidency in a return to the "patronal president" paradigm. Thus, while decentralization could be critical to breaking the cycle of "patronal presidencies" in Ukraine, the remaining structures that have facilitated this cycle could also serve to undermine the success of decentralization reforms.

In this context, various actors within the country are judging proposed decentralization reforms not only in terms of their ability to facilitate increased localization of power, but also in terms of their impact on the balance of power at the national level. For example, a variety of experts and political actors in the country have expressed concern with the initial constitutional amendments proposed by President Poroshenko due to what they perceive as their potential to lead the country back to a "patronal presidential" model. Poroshenko's amendments propose a system where units of local self-governance are empowered and given the resources needed to carry out their responsibilities, and they also include a strong "representative of the president" on the local level who is meant to provide oversight of local self-governance and ensure their actions are in compliance with national law.

Such national oversight is critical to the success of decentralization, ensuring that the reform does not lead to abuses of power at the local level or the weakening of the overall state, which is already threatened by intense conflict in the east of the country. While the authorities and oversight of the proposed local "presidential representatives" have not yet been fully outlined in law, some in the country worry that powerful interest groups may again seek to assert their interests through the presidency via this institution. Furthermore, critics assert that Poroshenko's proposed amendments to the constitution include other reforms that strengthen the presidency's influence over a number of key positions (Head of the National Bank, SBU, Prosecutor General, Anti-monopoly Committee, the State Property Fund, State Committee for Television and Radio Broadcasting, State Bureau of Investigations). Whether or not these are legitimate concerns, they are issues that must be ironed out in the final reform plans to ensure that decentralization has widespread support within Ukraine's varied political and economic elite. Without such support, the reforms could easily be derailed by any number of political forces.

During the assessment, most interviewees suggested that the existing parliament of Ukraine did not support these amendments. Even the coalition of parties within the parliament that has ratified the new government and generally supports the president (*Batkivshchyna*, *UDAR* and *Svoboda*) has criticized the amendments and wants to propose its own versions. However, recent developments have further complicated this situation. The *UDAR* and *Batkivshchyna* factions in the parliament have withdrawn from the coalition that had run the *Verkhovna Rada*, and Poroshenko has responded by announcing new parliamentary elections for October 2014. Poroshenko hopes that this will produce a more reform-minded parliament, but he also runs the risk that a new parliament will support his goals even less than the existing deputies.

Most importantly for this assessment, the present political economy in Ukraine creates three critical risks for the success of decentralization reform. First, the present flux in the political system, including the formation of a new parliament, could lead to decentralization reforms being significantly slowed down and perhaps even failing again as they did in 2006-2008. Depending upon the composition of the new parliament, there may continue to be serious opposition to plans for decentralization, at least until the functions and chain of command of the representative of central authorities on the local level is better defined. Second, the legacy of informal institutions of power in Ukraine will continue to pose a potential threat to the successful implementation of effective, accountable, and substantive decentralization reforms. By dismantling the previous vertical power structures that allowed powerful interest groups to exert extraordinary economic and political influence through the presidency, decentralization could allow for more resources to remain within localities and considerably limit the possibilities of high-level graft as seen in Yanukovych's presidency. However, many of those who would be called upon to approve such decentralization reforms and implement them may have incentives to not dismantle the previous vertical power system. Finally, the conflict in eastern Ukraine and the uncertainty of its outcome will inevitably slow down full implementation of reforms, at least until an agreement has been reached that fully brings all of eastern Ukraine back into the state system of the country.

II. METHODOLOGY

This assessment employed a mixed-methodology that included desk research, semi-structured interviews with key stakeholders, and focus groups with citizens who are not directly involved in the reform. The field research was conducted between July 7 and August 1, 2014. The assessment team traveled to a total of seven cities to conduct its research: Kyiv, Kharkiv, Zaporizhzhya, Odessa, Lviv, Ivano-Frankivsk, and Ternopil.

Semi-Structured Interviews

The assessment team conducted semi-structured interviews with central and local government officials, local experts, and civil society actors (See Appendix I for a full list of interviewees). With most interviews, excluding some with government officials and international donors, the assessment team asked a set group of questions designed to answer the three major research questions provided by the USAID mission (see Appendix II for interview protocol). The team then entered the answers to these questions into a database in order to generate quantitative data that could be disaggregated by stakeholder type, location, gender, and other dimensions (see Appendix III for the data-set). Additionally, the interviews would follow-up with more in-depth questions appropriate to the stakeholder with whom they were conducted, leading to a substantial amount of qualitative information regarding the three primary research questions.

In total the team conducted over fifty interviews with stakeholders, and quantitative data was collected for a total of forty-four. The largest samples of interviewees were in Kyiv, Kharkiv, and Lviv (See Graph I). The gender distribution of interviewees was decidedly skewed towards men, with about 84% of interviewees being men (see Graph II). This gender imbalance did not reflect a bias of the assessment team; rather, it was indicative of the degree to which primary stakeholders in the reform process (especially government officials and experts) were mostly male. Civil society actors were more evenly distributed by gender, but even in that sector, the assessment team found that most NGO activists working on issues of government accountability were male. Thus, the gender distribution of interviews is suggestive of a larger problem regarding gendered participation in politics in Ukraine. In virtually every local administration we visited, we found that the higher officials were men, and women were mostly relegated to lower-level administrative duties. The distribution of stakeholder type had a large number of civil society actors, but also included a significant number of local experts and local government officials (see Graph III). Given the difficulty of obtaining meetings with national government officials, they are less represented, and some of their interviews were not included in the quantitative data collection due to the formal nature of the meetings. Donor interviews were not included in the quantitative data collection.

Graph I: Location of Interviewees for Quantitative Data

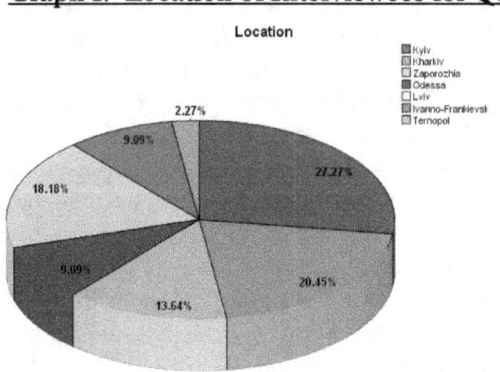

Graph II: Gender Distribution of Interviewees for Quantitative Data

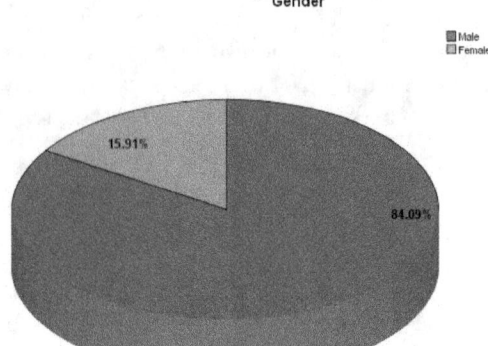

Gender

■ Male
□ Female

15.91%

84.09%

Graph III: Stakeholder Distribution of Interviewees for Quantitative Data

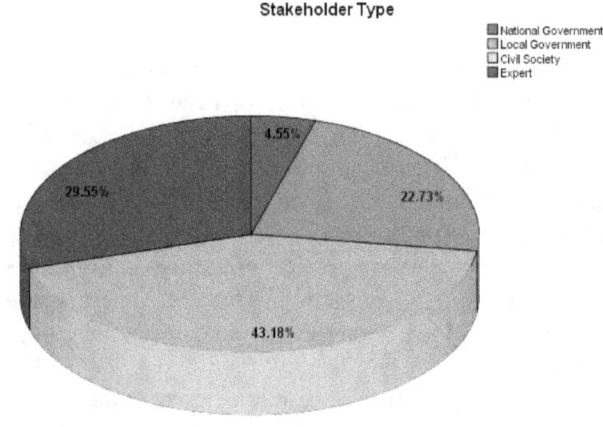

Stakeholder Type

■ National Government
□ Local Government
□ Civil Society
■ Expert

4.55%

22.73%

29.55%

43.18%

Citizen Focus Groups

The assessment team felt that it was critical to include citizen focus groups in the research given that successful decentralization will require substantial citizen buy-in and increased citizen participation in local decision-making. As a result, the team hired a commercial marketing firm, InMind Inc., with whom the team leader had previously worked, to organize and transcribe seven focus groups in four separate cities. Focus groups brought together local inhabitants who do not work in NGOs, the government, or journalism and are not political party activists. In this sense, they represent a constituency that is usually not consulted by international donors working on governance issues, but it is also a constituency that government is intended to serve. Furthermore, each focus group was equally distributed by gender and reflected the general economic spread of the population in question. Focus groups were also conducted by age co-hort, with two focus groups done with 20-29 year-olds, three with 30-45 year-olds, and two with 46-65 year-olds. These were spread across the cities of Kyiv (one group 20-29 and one group 46-65), Kharkiv (one group 30-45 and one group 46-65), Odessa (one group 20-29 and one group 30-45), and Lviv (one group 30-45). The focus groups provided particularly important insight into issues of local governance efficiency and corruption as well as an understanding of how citizens relate to the concept of decentralization and increased local authority. Appendix IV includes the full transcripts of all focus groups, and Appendix V includes a summary of findings put together by InMind. The assessment team's analysis of the focus groups is provided in the findings section of the report.

III. FINDINGS

Political Environment for Reform: Opportunities and Challenges

Reform Plans

The current crisis in Ukraine demands large-scale reform that can move the country towards effective and stable governance and provide for the country's citizens while also addressing the regional tensions that have been inflamed through the conflict in the east. These reforms should modernize Ukrainian society and create effective public institutions while also ensuring that local regions feel a part of the Ukrainian state regardless of which party controls the central government or who is president. The most critical of these reforms is decentralization and the empowerment and financing of local government as the primary unit of government administering public services and facilitating local development. Experts, non-governmental organizations, the wider population and the government are all aware of the need to immediately adopt such reforms.

As was already noted above, Ukraine has a long history of decentralization reforms, which have mostly been unrealized. Among past reform attempts, those proposed in 2006-08 are the most relevant to the present situation. In 2006 Roman Bezsmertnyi, then Deputy Prime Minister of Ukraine during the presidency of Viktor Yushchenko, developed a local government reform package that has not yet been implemented. This reform package has served as the main model for the decentralization reforms presently being proposed in the country. The main points of the reform package proposed by Bezsmertnyi were outlined in the draft law *On the territorial system of Ukraine* developed in 2006. This law called for the establishment of a three-level administrative-territorial system in Ukraine that would consist of communities (*hromada*), districts (*rayons*) and regions (*oblasts*). Additionally, it outlined that this system should comply with the subsidiarity principle that has become a central aspect of European decentralized governance. This principal suggests that the central government should only play a coordinating and oversight role in the daily activities of local governance by supporting and holding accountable local governmental bodies, which are afforded the primary role in local decision-making in order to more effectively provide public services and direct local development.

According to Bezsmertnyi's plan, the *hromada* was to be the basic administrative level of governance and should consist of one or several inhabited localities. A *hromada* should have no less than 5000 inhabitants. The district (*rayon*) is an aggregate of several *hromada*s that is established to promote their interests. No less than 70000 people should inhabit any given district. Additionally, the draft law accounted for the existence of "district-towns," based on a *hromada* that contains at least one town with a population of no less than 70000 people. "District-towns" were not to be administratively a part of the districts in which they are located. Instead, they would directly engage with the *oblast* government, which represents a conglomerate of districts and "district towns." The draft also accounted for the recognition of "regional cities" if at least one city with a population of 750000 or more people is located in the *hromada* territory. A "regional city" is not administratively part of the region where it is located. Instead, it is supported directly by the national government.

The draft of the law *On the territorial system of Ukraine* assigned regional status to the cities with a special status (Kiev and Sevastopol), to the Autonomous Republic of Crimea, to *oblasts*, and to "regional cities." In the cities with a population of no less than 450000, the draft also called for the creation of districts within the city. The population of one district should be no less than 150000 people, and the city should contain no less than three districts. These districts were not to be regarded as independent administrative units.

The draft law also clearly outlined that the power of state administration should be minimal, allowing for local government established by locally elected officials. It calls for the complete abolishment of district state administrations, and it substantially reduces the powers of *oblasts*' state administrations, which are transformed into coordination and representational bodies. This reform package borrowed heavily from the Polish example, which is evident in such features as the scope of *hromada* powers, the proposed three-level administrative-territorial system, and the quantitative means of determining the dimensions of *hromada*, district, region, "regional cities" and "district-towns."

The reforms in this draft law were never adopted during the Yushchenko presidency largely because the re-drawing of the territorial levels of governance met with resistance from local populations. Many communities did not want to abandon their present village councils for larger units in the form of *hromadas*. In discussing this history with interviewees, numerous people outside of Kyiv noted that the failure to convince local populations of the structure was due to the fact that it was a decision being imposed from Kyiv, and they did not understand its purpose. Still, the concept of reducing the number of territorial units in Ukraine is a critical aspect of decentralization. Without establishing a minimal threshold of 5000 inhabitants for a *hromada*, the reform would likely be ineffective, especially in smaller rural villages that would not have the capacity to fulfill all needed administrative functions, particularly in such areas as education and health care, which were eventually to be decentralized to the *hromada* level. Furthermore, it would be likewise difficult for small rural villages to establish their own economic development strategies and to raise revenue.

Currently, a new decentralization plan is being drawn up that draws heavily from the plan originally spearheaded by Bezsmertnyi in 2006-08. In general, the new plan is almost identical to that described above with a few exceptions, which will be further discussed below. The proposed reforms in the current effort are outlined in two draft documents – the *Concept of Local Government and Territorial Organization of Power in Ukraine* (adopted by the Cabinet of Minister on April 1, 2014) and the draft of the law on amendments to the Constitution of Ukraine (#4178a).

The "concept" presupposes the amendment of the Constitution of Ukraine (CoU), but it also goes into more detail than the constitutional amendments. For example, the "concept" suggests concrete numbers of *hromada* and *rayons* for the new territorial-administrative structure of the country. In place of the some 15000 *hromada* presently existing in the country, it proposes consolidating them into approximately 1200. Likewise, in place of the some 500 *rayons* presently in existence, it suggests consolidating them into approximately 100. To realize these and other plans in the "concept," it is required to change articles #133, #142 and #119 of the Constitution. Changes to article #133 of the CoU would introduce the notion of *hromada* as the basic unit of Ukraine's administrative-territorial system along the same lines as in Bezsmertnyi's plan. The current version of the legislation uses the notion of *territorial hromada*, which refers to existing village inhabitants or the voluntary union of several villages, *poseloks* (small village-type settlements adjacent to villages or towns) and one town. The revised concept of *hromada* is based on the three-level administrative-territorial model of Poland, in which *hromada* is analogous to the *gmina* territorial unit. The introduction of this revised concept of *hromada* is critical to the formation of the three-level administrative-territorial system of Ukraine, the realization of the subsidiarity principle and the clear division of administrative powers. The current version of article #133 of the CoU does not provide a clear definition of the different administrative-territorial levels of governance or their respective roles (it only lists the components of the administrative-territorial system).

Changes to article #142 of the CoU seek to establish the material basis for local government development. It proposes transferring a portion of national taxes to local governments and adopting a formula to ensure that the volume of financial assets of local governments should correspond to their authorities (envisaged by the laws and the CoU). This will be the most critical aspect of realizing effective decentralization reform, and it is expected that much work will need to be done to design the proper distribution of taxes and authority for local revenue collection as well as the system for subsidizing local budgets in poorer regions, even after the constitution has been changed to allow for the material basis for local government development.

Finally, changes to article #119 of the CoU would abolish local-level state administration bodies and replace them with local representative bodies appointed by *hromada* councils. These local representative bodies would undertake the work of local governance and answer primarily to the locally elected councils, which appoint them. Additionally, a local "representative of the president" (and his or her staff) would conduct oversight over the work of local governance to ensure that these local representative officials are not in violation of the Constitution or the laws of the state of Ukraine, coordinate operations of state inspections' offices at the local level, and coordinate operations of national-level executive state agencies on the local level. Key powers of *oblast* and *rayon* state administrations, in essence, would be transferred to *hromadas*, *rayons* and *oblasts*, and the role of the president's representative locally is to ensure that these new powers and responsibilities are not abused. This structure is proposed as a check on local governments, including as a means to prevent local corruption and separatism. The proposed institution of the "representative of the president" is based on the Polish and French administrative-territorial model and is roughly analogous to the institution of the *voivode* in Poland and the institution of the *perfect* in France.

In the reform process thus far, it is the changes to article #119 that have been most controversial. While the experts who had worked on the original draft of constitutional amendments had anticipated that representatives of the national government on the local level would answer to the Cabinet of Ministers and the Prime Minister, the draft of the law on the amendments to the Constitution of Ukraine (#4178a) that was presented to parliament proposed that the representatives of the national government on the local level be both appointed by and accountable to the presidency exclusively. This has raised concerns among some that the institution could disrupt the balance of political powers at the national level in Ukraine and could even be used to return the country to the "patronal presidency" form of government that has characterized Ukraine since independence.

While the institution of the "president's representative" is similar to the institutions of the *voivode* in Poland and *prefect* institution in France, the "dual-executive powers" at the national level in Ukraine complicate the institution's implementation in the Ukrainian context. Ukraine since 2005 has had a "dual executive" model of power with a president elected by popular vote and a Prime Minister who must be approved by the parliament. As was already discussed in this report's "political economy analysis," this model was meant to put a check on all-powerful presidencies, and presidents have in turn frequently sought to weaken the Prime Ministers with whom they work in order to empower themselves. In this context, some experts and political actors worry that the institution of the "president's representative" on the local level proposed in constitutional amendments could disrupt the balance of power between the presidency and the Prime Minister if this position answers exclusively to the president and that such a configuration of power could further reinforce Ukraine's unstable cycle of powerful and weakened presidents. Even if Poroshenko may not have reason to use the institution to empower his office vis-à-vis the cabinet of ministers, there is no guarantee that his successor, or other powerful interest groups in the country, would not. Regardless of whether such concerns are justified, it will be critical that the final iteration of reforms further clarify the role and accountability of the "representative of the president" locally to alleviate the concerns of various stakeholders and to ensure that the reforms are backed by a broad group of different political forces in the country.

Although some concerns exist about the model of decentralization presently proposed, the local governance reform "concept" and the proposed constitutional amendments still represent an excellent basis for redefining the relationships between local governments and the central government, and they have the potential to make government in Ukraine both more effective and less susceptible to state capture by a small group of powerful political and economic actors. More important than any misgivings about the present model being proposed are the questions of how the political process may change the form of decentralization ultimately adopted by the parliament and whether proposed decentralization will be left unrealized as occurred in 2006-08. In this context, it will be critical that all political actors involved in debating and formulating the reform's final version via legislative and constitutional changes be ready to set aside their own political aspirations for the national good and adopt a system that empowers local governments, ensures their accountability both to citizens and to the national government, and reinforces the accountability of national level state officials and the checks and balances of Ukraine's present political system.

Opportunities and Constraints to Reform

A key prerequisite for successful decentralization reform is consensus and demand for change among the population, as well as accumulation of social capital in society, which can be leveraged for the implementation of the reforms. These factors are largely present in Ukraine at the moment. The "EuroMaidan" movement has helped to facilitate a relatively strong consensus in the country regarding the urgency of Ukraine's integration into the European community, and recent Russian aggression towards Ukraine has helped to strengthen this consensus. Both the "EuroMaidan" movement and the actions of the Russian Federation in Ukraine have also activated social capital in the country in unprecedented ways. A rise in patriotism facilitated in part by the fear of external threats has helped to bridge many traditionally divisive cleavages in society, including religion (cooperation between Muslim and Orthodox churches during the Crimea conflict), identity politics (cooperation of far-right and Jewish organizations over accusations of fascism), military-civilian relations (creation of voluntary military units and the overwhelming volunteer support for the military campaign in the east of the country), relations between security forces and citizens (despite confrontations during the "EuroMaidan" protests, there is now increased cooperation between *siloviki* and civic activists), etc. Additionally, there appears to be a broad consensus among primary stakeholders that decentralization is one of the most important reforms for Ukraine to address in the short-term. When asked by the assessment team if decentralization reforms were likely to be successful, for example, many stakeholder interviewees merely said, "they *must* be successful." Furthermore, when asked if they understood that real reform might entail difficulties in their lives and would take time, most stakeholders suggested that they were ready to weather short to medium term difficulties for longer term goals.

This support for decentralization reform among most stakeholders and the wider population as well as the increased social capital apparent across Ukrainian society certainly represent opportunities for facilitating successful outcomes. Among other things, the consensus on the need for reform has helped to establish a broad coalition of civil society organizations, which are coordinating amongst themselves in order to provide government officials with the technical and legislative materials required to establish successful decentralization. Additionally, there appears to be political will at high levels in the national government for these reforms, both within the presidency and in the Ministry of Regional Development. Most civil society actors interested in decentralization reform, for example, view the Minister of Regional Development, Volodymyr Groisman, as a colleague whom they trust to advocate for this reform. However, these factors alone do not guarantee the success of the reforms. In addition to these opportunities, there exist many limitations that constrain the successful adoption and implementation of real decentralization reforms in Ukraine.

The largest constraints to the realization of these reforms is the potential that powerful political forces in the country, on both the national and local level, may oppose the reform's ultimate adoption and implementation. As has already been mentioned, many national level political forces are suspicious of the reform's potential to empower the president vis-à-vis the Prime Minister through the "president's representative" on the local level. Additionally, political elites at the local level are suspicious that the "president's representative" on the local level will serve to unduly exert Kyiv's will on local governments. In reality, it is a standard practice of unitary states to oversee local government compliance with the national legislation, and such oversight is critical to curbing graft and the abuse of power by local officials. The question will be how the powers of these "president's representatives" will be defined and to whom they will be accountable. Several local government representatives with whom we spoke, for example, worried that the position could be used to exert undue influence from the presidency at the local level and that the "president's representative" would be able to easily halt local government actions by politically motivated court cases questioning the constitutionality of those actions. Since the support of local political elites will be essential for the success of the decentralization reforms, it will be important that these concerns are addressed in the process of realizing the reform.

Similarly, the reform could face opposition from local elites due to the proposed administrative-territorial reform, which will greatly reduce the number of local councils by consolidating existing governmental units into larger ones. As already noted, such resistance was a major reason behind the failure of the previous attempt to establish serious decentralization reforms in 2006-08. Presently, the local elites at various levels of administrative hierarchy take advantage of public posts and economic influence to extract resources and protect their vested interests. The consolidation of *hromadas* and other administrative-territorial units implies both the reduction of such administrative positions locally and a decrease of rent sources from such positions, especially given that the proposed reform envisages the expansion of fiscal and budget powers locally. The concentration of budgetary authority locally will inevitably create enhanced local awareness of graft and its negative impact on local communities, making it more difficult for local rent-seeking elites to practice corrupt activities, especially when local government positions will be appointed by a locally elected council.

On the one hand, as already discussed previously, this is a critical part of decentralization reform, especially for smaller rural villages. If such smaller villages are not consolidated into larger governance units, they will not have the human capital, capacity, or resources to practice serious self-governance. On the other hand, the anticipated resistance that such plans will likely encounter if implemented has made some stakeholders who are promoting reform seek alternative means to establish larger governance units. A recent draft law *On unification of territorial hromadas*, for example, makes provisions for the voluntary associations (or cooperation agreements) of *hromada*s. This would allow some villages to seek ways to establish joint governance structures without the unification of territorial units. While such a resolution of this problem may help some isolated rural communities realize self-governance, unless a majority of rural communities in the country undertake such unifying measures on their own, it is unlikely that Ukraine can uniformly decentralize. Furthermore, it is very possible that those attempts to voluntarily unify rural communities will be sabotaged by local elites whose interests would be threatened by such actions.

Whether these fears on the part of local political actors are justified will depend upon how the reform is ultimately articulated and implemented. There are various ways that the powers and accountability structures surrounding the "president's representative" on the local level can ensure that this institution neither strengthens the hand of the president vis-à-vis the Prime Minister nor allows the undue influence of the national government over local decision making. Similarly, there are ways to structure the consolidation of *hromadas* and *rayons* so that the borders of existing territories do not change, but are merely represented by councils overseeing governance for a combination of the existing villages or districts. These are all issues that can and should be resolved in the further articulation of the reform plan with the participation of both local level and national level political actors. The primary danger facing the reform is that various political actors, who maintain suspicions that the reform will not serve their personal interests, could derail the process of finalizing the structure and implementation of the reform. Thus, the upcoming discussions and negotiations about the reform in the new parliament that will be elected in late October will be critical to successful decentralization.

These negotiations could be particularly intense regarding the parts of eastern Ukraine presently outside Kyiv's full control given that these regions will only buy into the reform if it ensures that they will be empowered locally to make their own decisions without extensive intervention from Kyiv. At present, it is impossible to forecast how the conflict in eastern Ukraine will end and when. However, if the regions of Donetsk and Luhansk do fully return to become integral parts of the Ukrainian state, one can expect that effective and extensive decentralization will be critical to integrating these regions' populations back into Ukrainian society. While it is virtually impossible to know authoritatively about the attitudes of the people of Donbas towards Kyiv given the present information war and the isolation of those who have remained in the region, journalists' reports suggest that even those who have not actively supported the separatists have lost much faith in the Kyiv government given the lack of resolution in the conflict. If these people remain citizens of Ukraine, much work will need to be done to persuade them that they have an important voice in the country and that the state will provide for them. In this context, decentralization has the potential to be a critical aspect of reintegrating the Donbas region into a new Ukraine, but, at the same time, the buy-in of the people of Donbas regarding the reform will be essential for successful decentralization.

Local self-government reform and power decentralization will allow the people of Donbas to have increased agency in the rebuilding and redefinition of their local societies. If implemented well and held accountable, newly empowered local governments should also serve to improve the quality of public services available to people. The main governance problem previously experienced in Donbas was the synthesis between Ukraine's centralized administrative-territorial system and the strong positions of regional elites, who controlled key assets and occupied main offices in the region. This led to the establishment of a quite centrally controlled society where local citizens had little voice and the state was not very accountable to a constituency other than the local elites. In this situation, corruption flourished, and most people saw limited benefits from the fruits of local industrial production and natural resource extraction. While well implemented decentralization could address such problems, local support for such reform will depend upon the degree to which they truly limit Kyiv's influence over local decision-making regarding the daily activities of government and public services while also facilitating locally elected governments that are accountable to citizens and transparent regarding state revenues and expenditures. Furthermore, the issue of the status of Russian language in this region, both in terms of official use and education, will likely be something that most citizens in Donbas will want to be decided locally. Such an outcome will necessitate a carefully crafted role for the "presidential representatives" on the local level that both ensures these regions are integrated into Ukrainian society and accountable to the national government while given substantive latitude in their self-governance.

Another constraint to successful decentralization reform is the widespread corruption in the country that emerges from the pervasiveness of client-patron networks. Corruption in Ukraine has been an institutional phenomenon both at local and central levels for a long time, and it is unreasonable to believe that new configurations of local governance accompanied by the empowerment of government bodies on the local level will quickly reduce corruption. While many of the stakeholders with whom we spoke noted that they expected decentralization to eventually reduce corruption, most also admitted that this would take some time. Furthermore, while decentralization should theoretically deter centralized corruption networks, if elections to local councils continue to include half of the seats being chosen through closed party lists, it is likely that many local deputies will still find themselves beholden to national patron-client networks that are manifested through the political party system. This will likely continue at least some opportunities for national-level corruption schemes that involve local political power. In this context, it is critical that decentralization reforms be coupled with serious anti-corruption efforts that can demonstrate to citizens that the empowerment of local governmental structures can make governance more effective and positively impact their daily lives.

Additionally, one should not ignore the constraints placed on decentralization reform by the continued conflict in the eastern Donbas region of Ukraine. Although the reform could be conducted in the rest of Ukraine prior to a reunification with Donbas, such implementation of decentralization will lead to non-uniform reform, the character of which will not include recommendations from the Donbas region. Furthermore, the continuation of the conflict in the region and the escalation of Russia's involvement in it is also obviously consuming substantial state resources, both financially and politically, and it is likely that its continuation will force subsequent delays in the implementation of substantive reforms not only in Donbas, but throughout the country.

Another hindrance to decentralization reform will be the struggle over fiscal decentralization. The reforms cannot be successful without a substantial re-orientation of public finances in a way that provides units of local self-governance with the resources they require to fulfill their enhanced responsibilities. Such fiscal restructuring will require substantial legislative changes, particularly in the country's Tax Code. As one might expect, such changes to the present system will likely be the most controversial and involve the broadest array of vested economic interests. To date, little has been done to fully outline what the actual system for fiscal decentralization will look like, but this is the aspect of decentralization reform that will be the most critical to ensuring a real re-distribution of state power to the local level. If Ukraine follows the model of many developing countries and politically decentralizes without aligning public financing with the newly empowered local authorities, the outcome will be largely an empty reform that changes little in the country.

Finally, although most citizens and major stakeholders are in favor of decentralization reform, it is unclear whether the different political parties in the present and future parliament will be able to come to a consensus on how these reforms should progress. Given that full reform will require not only changing the constitution, but also amending a substantial number of legislative acts, the parliament will remain an indispensible player in the reform's success. Furthermore, the reform runs the risk of failure if certain legislative acts are successfully amended while others are not. Such a situation could lead to a system that cannot effectively operate, thus quickly turning citizens against the concept of decentralization as a whole.

While this section has generally outlined more constraints than opportunities for decentralization, it is noteworthy that many local government officials and experts told the assessment team that increased decentralization was possible even without substantial legislative changes. At least in larger towns and cities, Ukrainian units of self-governance already have more authority to govern locally than they employ at present. In this context, some fiscal decentralization could be achieved without substantial legislative changes, and local authorities can take over responsibilities that are presently controlled by the central government regardless of whether there is constitutional change. A good example of the potential to embrace increased decentralization without changing the constitution or enacting new legislation is Ternopil's initiative to create a municipal police force. As the head of the Ternopil city council told us, the local city government undertook this reform unilaterally, and the Ministry of Internal Affairs now tolerates it. Thus, if reforms are seriously delayed, USAID may also consider interventions that can enhance decentralization without corresponding legislative mechanisms. At the very least, such projects could demonstrate the potential of serious reform and hopefully increase demand for it. Unfortunately, such work would not be very successful in small rural communities, which lack the resources, human capital, and capacity to take on additional governance responsibilities.

Prospects for Reform

At present, it is impossible to provide a confident assessment of the prospects that decentralization reform will be carried out in Ukraine in the near future. On the one hand, there is substantial political will and popular support for the reform. On the other hand, there are numerous constraints to its successful implementation. Most of those involved in drawing up plans for the reform agree that it should be implemented quickly before more centralized power is entrenched and popular interest in the reform wanes. In particular, most experts and national-level politicians feel that the window of opportunity for implementation of the reform is before the local elections planned for the fall of 2015. This makes sense given that it would be problematic to elect new local councils and mayors before changing their authorities and responsibilities. Furthermore, it would be impossible to implement territorial consolidation after the elections have taken place, since such consolidation would inevitably change the electoral map, particularly in rural areas, not to mention vastly reduce the number of local councils. If Ukraine does succeed in putting all reforms in place prior to the 2015 local elections, it will be able to initiate newly elected officials into the new system of local self-governance.

Additionally, such quick implementation of reforms may help to facilitate a de-escalation and peaceful settlement of the violent conflict in the Donbas region. Even if the reform is first implemented elsewhere in the country prior to a full cessation of the conflict in Donbas, Kyiv will be able to demonstrate to the people of Donbas that it is serious about reducing national state authorities and enhancing local authority. This would likely make the region's acceptance of reintegration with the rest of the country easier as local people realize that being a part of Ukraine brings local empowerment and potentially more effective governance. Likely one of the most controversial issues under such a scenario will be whether decentralization reforms will allow certain regions to make Russian at least a second state language and a language of instruction in schools. While many western Ukrainians may oppose providing such authority over questions of language to local governments, it would be welcomed by the people of Donbas and would likely be an attractive incentive to re-integrate into the Ukrainian state.

However, such a rapid deployment of decentralization reforms also carries with it some risks. First, it may require certain compromises, especially regarding two critical, yet controversial aspects of the reform: the consolidation of administrative-territorial units and the mechanism of oversight employed by the national government over local governments (presently articulated through the institution of the local "president's representative." If these critical aspects of the reform are instituted haphazardly in the interest of expediency, they could become highly politicized in the context of the October 2015 local elections, perhaps even leading to conflicts that could disrupt the political process.

Another risk to rapid implementation of reforms is that it requires the amendment of articles #119, 133 and 142 of the Constitution. To accomplish this, a minimum of 300 parliamentary votes is required from a group of new deputies who have yet to be elected. As noted above, the alternative to changing the constitution is proceeding with reforms exclusively based on the amendments of current legislation, including Tax and Budget Codes. In this case, local fiscal and budget powers may be extended to units of local self-governance, and this could even foster the voluntary consolidation of *hromada*s, at least in some instances. Unfortunately, such an approach to reforms would be less sustainable and more susceptible to a return to the status quo even after partial successes.

Despite the risks involved in quickly implementing decentralization reforms, most stakeholders with whom the assessment team met suggested that there was not really another alternative if Ukraine is to survive its present crisis and begin a new phase of democratization. Indeed, if the reform is successfully implemented, it has the potential to vastly change the Ukrainian system and break the cycle of the "patronal president" system. While it is unlikely to eradicate corruption, or even reduce it in the near term, it has the potential to transform the architecture of the country's corruption system. A transfer of tangible fiscal and budget powers to local governments will mean the weakening of central power structures as the regulator of financial flows and corruption rents. In turn, it will likely lead to the establishment of local rent-extracting pyramids.

Although this could merely replace one network of corruption with another, it may at least generate more local economic development rather than allowing high-level graft to siphon wealth to Kyiv. This is because the main source of profits for rent-seeking entrepreneurs is not only protection rent (incomes from the politico-juridical protection of business), but also rent from large-scale economic projects (e.g. in construction and infrastructure development). Thus, the weakening of central fiscal and budget powers will likely contribute to the proliferation of such projects at the local level. In other words, instead of large nationwide projects (like EURO-2012), we may witness numerous local economic projects, at least in "rent-intensive" sectors of the economy.

The long-term hope for such a transformation is that it eventually leads to increased accountability from local governments since local corruption activities are much easier to identify and expose than those at the national level. "Watchdog" civic groups and investigative journalists in Ukraine have become more active, brave, and professional in recent years, and they are capable mechanisms for oversight of local governance and especially of the use of public funds. The success of such organizations as the civic movement *Chesno*, *Automaidan*, and the journalistic investigations of *Tvi* and *Gromads'ke TV* may stimulate the growth of similar groups on the local level which are able to better control local authorities and consequently contribute to the overall decrease of corruption in the political system of Ukraine.

Local Capacity to Carry Out Reforms

Capacity of Local Officials to Undertake Increased Responsibilities

One of the most critical challenges facing decentralization reforms in Ukraine is the lack of human capital and capacity to effectively administer the duties of governance at the local level. A giant and expanding administrative bureaucracy that has continually grown in size since 1991 despite Ukraine's steadily decreasing population exacerbates this problem. Since 1991, the number of villages in the country grew by 348 units, and the number of village council by 1067 units. In more than 6000 *hromada*s, the population is less than 3000 people, in 4809 *hromada*s - less than 1000 people and in 1129 *hromada*s – there are less than 500 inhabitants. Most of these underpopulated *hromada*s even lack executive bodies, which can perform governmental functions. Furthermore, a substantial number of these villages bring in virtually no revenue, resulting in about 70-90% of the local budget being subsidized by central budget authorities.

These small rural communities have virtually no capacity to implement self-governance, and it would not make sense to build such capacity as long as they remain their present size. If the consolidation of *hromada*s takes place as outlined in proposed reforms, however, one can envision a need for substantial capacity building for the governance bodies that oversee several of these former *hromada*.

Although local capacity for the self-governance of larger consolidated *hromada* likely varies markedly by location, most people with whom we spoke suggested that the needs for capacity building at this local level of governance will be significant. In particular, it is important that local councils gain the capacity to effectively run meetings, debate and formulate local policies and budgets as well as partake in long-term strategic planning. Since most of these activities have formerly not been conducted at this level of governance, it is unlikely that many if any of the council members will have prior experience with them. In short, if reforms are realized, including the consolidation of *hromadas*, the new local self-government's elected officials will need plenty of assistance if they are to successfully fulfill their new responsibilities.

Most interviewees also suggested that there were similar capacity-building needs at the district or *rayon* level. However, the elected district councils will likely have less of a governance role than will local *hromada*. In fact, the role of both *rayon* and *oblast* councils will most likely be limited to promoting regional development and coordination between *hromada* while the daily duties of making substantive decisions about public services and other local issues will be the responsibility of the *hromada*. Assuming the roles outlined above for these units of governance, capacity building needs at the *rayon* and *oblast* level should mostly include more competency in regional development strategic plan development and in working with the variety of *hromada* within their jurisdiction. But, it should be noted that the roles of *rayons* and *oblasts* remain poorly articulated in the reform plans and still must be further articulated before reforms are fully implemented.[4]

At the level of "district-towns," interviewees suggested that there presently exists a decent level of capacity for governance, but it has been developed around the former centralized system of state power. Thus, in such towns, one can anticipate that the level of capacity building needs will be similar to those on the *hromada* level. By contrast, most interviewees felt that the capacity of officials in "regional cities" was already quite high. In fact, one expert, who has been one of the primary authors of the reform plans, told the assessment team that successful reform would change little at the level of "regional cities," with the exception of giving them more access to resources. According to this expert, the real goal of the reform will be to invest the same level of authority now afforded "regional cities" in local *hromada*.

As already noted several times, state decentralization and the empowerment of local self-governance authorities requires substantial fiscal decentralization that is premised on a new budget model. Unfortunately, the assessment team found little evidence that the primary authors of the reform were focused on the details of how this new budget model would operate. Likely, it will require substantial changes to the Budget and Tax Codes, allowing for local revenue generation and for a mechanism at the national level to redistribute funds in order to subsidize underdeveloped *hromada*. This system will be even further complicated if education and health care also become financed and managed at the local level. Regardless of the details of this new budget model, its implementation will require significant capacity building at all levels of governance to ensure that revenues are collected and expended effectively and without graft. This will be a large undertaking that will likely require a massive training program to be implemented throughout the country.

Overall, therefore, the assessment team anticipates that the capacity-building needs on the local level, particularly in *hromada* councils, will be massive if reforms are fully implemented. That said, as

---

[4] The authors of the reform plans still need to clearly articulate the different roles of both *oblasts* and *rayons*. The key issue is whether these entities should be understood as a community of people who inhabit it, or as a community of communities located in this region. In the first case (if a *rayons* and *oblasts* are defined as a community), they should receive additional political leverage that allows the to put forward a number of political demands, such as referendum initiatives. In the second case (as a community of communities), one should secure communal representation in the *oblast* and *rayon* councils, which will result in the greater number of deputies. These different roles are suggestive of different capacity needs.

already noted, the reform plans still poorly articulate the full scope of authorities that will be relegated to different levels of governance. Thus, the full scope of capacity building needs will depend upon the clear articulation of the spheres of competency at each level of the proposed administrative-territorial system of Ukraine. Additionally, the role of different levels of governance regarding the status of local collective property must be clarified since such property is potentially a significant source of revenue. If *hromadas* are given ownership of such land and property, for example, local councils will need to build their capacity for managing property assets as well.

To conclude, it is worth reiterating that the above capacity-building needs are premised on a certain interpretation of the actual roles and responsibilities relegated to different levels of governance through the reform. Yet, the reform plans do not fully articulate these roles and responsibilities, and changes to the reform as it goes through the political process of being adopted could completely alter our present assumptions about the needs at each level of governance. Thus, before the reform is fully implemented, several outstanding questions must be answered to determine the full scope of capacity-building needs at the local level. These include:

- A clear definition and delineation of powers and competencies to be delegated to the *hromada*, *rayon* and *oblast* levels;
- A clear articulation of the level of economic and administrative independence of *hromada*s;
- A detailed plan regarding the scope of taxes and levies that will form the local governments' budgets;
- A detailed plan regarding how the national budget will redistribute funds to assist *hromadas* with substantial revenue shortfalls, particularly with regards to funding for education and health care;
- A clearer definition of the status of *oblasts* and *rayons* as either communities of people, who inhabit this particular region, or, alternatively as communities of communities located in the region;

Capacity and Involvement of Civil Society in Local Governance

Ukrainian civil society has become more sophisticated in recent years, and it has also become both more politicized and broader in its constituency since the EuroMaidan protests began in November 2013. Almost in every location visited by the assessment team, interviewees noted that civil society had been critical in the organization of EuroMaidan protests around the country and subsequently in providing assistance to refugees from Crimea and eastern Ukraine and in raising money for the military. In Kyiv, civil society actors from analytical centers have played a substantial role in drawing up designs for decentralization and working with the Ministry of Regional Development to produce draft constitutional amendments and legislation intended to empower local self-governance. Furthermore, regional NGOs, especially in Oblast' centers, have worked with analytical centers in Kyiv to contribute to these efforts.

However, the assessment team found consistently that regional civil society groups had less capacity and resources to engage government than was the case in Kyiv. This phenomenon appears to be a product of donor organizations supporting national reform projects through larger NGOs in Kyiv, which subsequently sub-contract regional work to local organizations. The result has been that most stronger and resource-rich NGOs are in the capitol and focus on national-level policy issues and oversight. If the proposed decentralization reforms are implemented, there will be a much larger need for local civil society actors to do direct oversight of local governance and to provide analytical services to local councils in the same way Kyiv-based organizations have been accustomed to doing for national level oversight and analytical support in the past.

Interviews with stakeholders revealed that numerous mechanisms exist for citizen input into local governmental decision-making and oversight, including the civic advisory councils that are attached to both local councils and ministerial representatives on the local level, public hearings, and town hall meetings (See Graph IV). However, most interviewees suggested that these mechanisms had existed in most regions to date in a purely consultative manner that was more intended to demonstrate state interaction with citizens than to establish real oversight or input. In fact, when asked whether such mechanisms were sufficient to establish citizen input and oversight into local governance, only one interviewee responded affirmatively, and that was a representative of local government (See Graph V).

Although the *Party of Regions* under Yanukovych had mandated that local officials from the party engage with civil society groups, this interaction was usually not substantive and almost never included real oversight. In regions where other parties controlled local administrations, civil society groups reported similar experiences, even when the dominant parties had emerged from within civil society. This reality was reflected in the fact that political will was the most frequent explanation as to why there did not exist sufficient citizen oversight and input in matters of local governance. However, it was noteworthy that an equal number of responses from civil society actors noted that one of the reasons for a lack of citizen involvement was due to inadequate local capacity. In particular, many civil society actors stressed that few local organizations had the skills to conduct oversight over such technical issues as government expenditures and tender competitions. At the same time, they noted that the Freedom of Information law in place was working and that information on government activities was available to those who knew what to request.

Graph IV: How are civil society and citizens now involved in local governance decision-making and oversight?

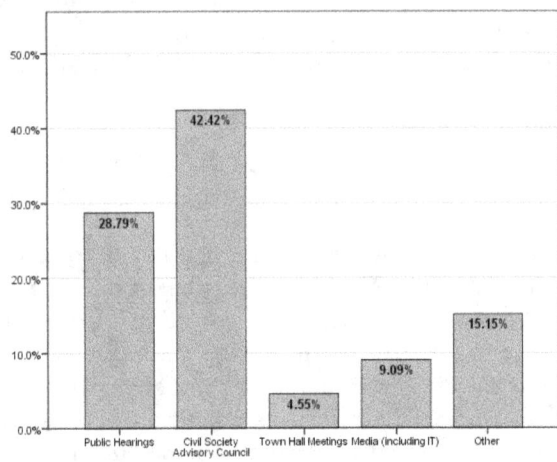

Graph V: Has this been sufficient? If not, what has constrained more robust engagement?

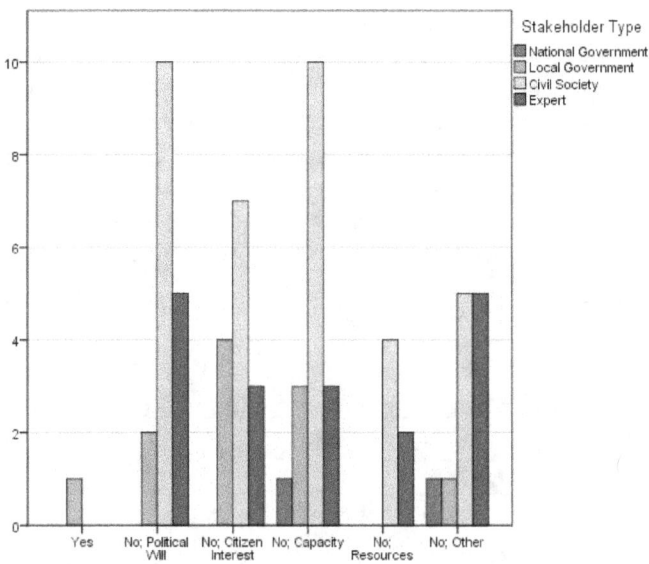

This situation is particularly concerning given the levels of corruption reported in Ukraine, and the experience the population recently endured with the extraordinary levels of top-level corruption under the Yanukovych government. While a slight majority of interviewees anticipated that decentralization would decrease corruption by hopefully dismantling the verticals of power that have long siphoned local money and resources off to Kyiv (See Graph VI), the overwhelming majority noted in further conversations that such an impact would depend substantially on increased citizen oversight on the local level. Civil society actors in particular noted that local political machines already operate in the larger oblast centers around the country that partake in corrupt activities, and a lack of local oversight would likely exacerbate this phenomenon regardless of what decentralization reforms are implemented.

Graph VI: How do you anticipate decentralization and the redistribution of power to local governments will impact corruption?

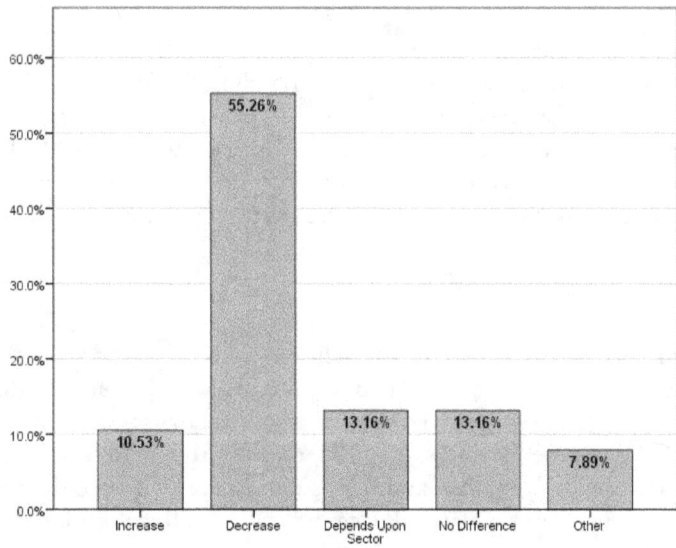

In this regard, most interviewees reiterated that successful decentralization would need to be accompanied by serious anti-corruption efforts including increased implementation of e-governance transparency and strong civil society oversight that is capable of using the information afforded by government transparency. Citizen focus groups reiterated this point, as most citizens equated better governance with a decrease in corruption. In stakeholder interviews, virtually all respondents (including government officials) suggested that they had witnessed or experienced corruption at the hands of the government, and most pointed to the activities related to land distribution, real estate, and construction as the most egregiously corrupt (See Graph VII). While they noted that most of the authority over these issues was put into the hands of national-level authorities under Yanukovych, they did not necessarily believe that merely bringing these responsibilities to the local level would resolve the problem.

Graph VII: Have you encountered corruption in your interactions with local government? If so, in what sphere of activities?

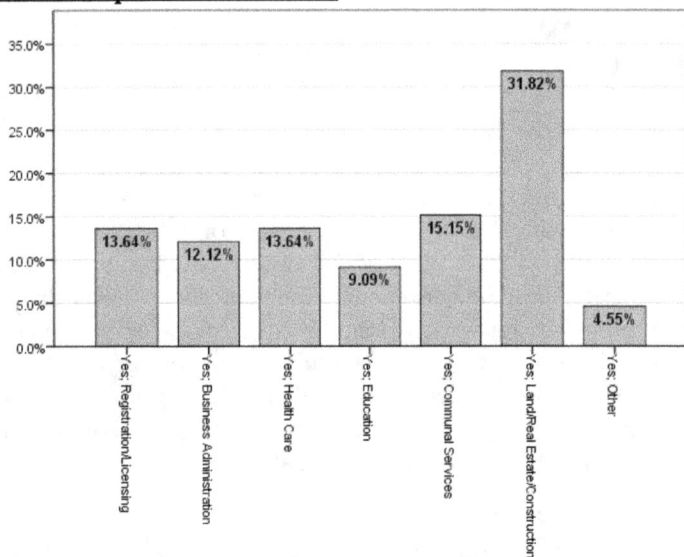

In this context, the assessment team found that support and capacity building for local "watchdog" organizations should be a critical aspect of donor engagement with decentralization reforms. This is already an area in which USAID has substantial experience and is well placed to support. At the same time, local analytical organizations should be supported as resources for local governments in order to help them research economic and social issues critical to local strategic planning.

Citizen Attitudes Towards Reforms

The realization of proposed decentralization reforms depends heavily on popular support. The lack of this support may result in the postponement of urgent, but potentially unpopular reforms. Furthermore, diverse popular sentiments during reform implementation frequently contribute to changes and amendments that affect its outcome. At the same time, reforms that address the most pressing problems of the population are usually embraced and fully supported. In this context, it is critical to understand the attitudes of citizens towards planned decentralization reforms and to better understand what would translate as more effective governance for them.

One of the most immediate findings from the focus groups we administered for this assessment in Kyiv, Kharkiv, Odessa and Lviv was that the citizenry of Ukraine neither trusts government nor expects it to provide quality services and protections for its people. Ukrainian citizens experience the structural crisis of state institutions and their excessive centralization on a daily basis in virtually all of their interactions with government institutions (health care, law enforcement, justice and education). Centralization gives rise to a large bureaucratic apparatus mired in corruption that only exacerbates the poor quality of government services. In general, citizens do not view the government as something that works in their service – they view government as predatory, corrupt, and invasive.

Still, most participants, with the exception of the 20-29 age co-hort, believed that this could change, and they were still willing to entertain reforms, which could improve their lives and restore their confidence in government. Furthermore, when asked about what local government services were delivered satisfactorily, they demonstrated a capacity to appreciate innovative changes. In Kharkiv, for example, focus group participants talked favorably about a "hot-line" instituted to request emergency services and to report state services that were not provided on request. In Lviv and Odessa, participants talked positively about the improvements they had experienced in receiving government documents, such as licenses and permits, through recently established one-stop service centers. Finally, most participants in all cities where focus groups were conducted demonstrated more trust in local government than in national government.

When asked about the most pressing local problems that they would like to see local government resolve, most participants in the focus groups named corruption, the lack of employment opportunities, and a general lack of economic development. This is important information because it suggests that the citizen participants would consider decentralization reform a positive development if it addressed these particular problems.

Again with the notable exception of those in their 20s, most participants demonstrated a nuanced understanding of the importance of decentralizing state power while recognizing that this was different than the establishment of "federalism." As one participant from the 30-45 age co-hort noted, "Decentralization with partial independence for the regions is optimal for Ukraine; the idea of federalization is not supported by the population – especially after the events in Crimea and in the East." Generally, participants suggested that decentralization of political power in Ukraine would help to address the country's problems of an excessively bureaucratic and ineffective state apparatus. While most participants were not under the illusion that decentralization would eradicate corruption, they did suggest that local corruption was easier for citizens to monitor and control than is national-level graft.

While most participants supported the idea of decentralization reforms, they also were poorly informed about its details. When participants were shown a "power-point" presentation outlining the reform, many were actually quite pleasantly surprised that the new government had such plans. Most participants were mildly optimistic and hoped that the proposed reforms could change conditions in the country for the better, but they were also quite cynical and inclined to believe that it probably would not. As one participant articulated using a popular phrase for unmet expectations, "we wanted it to be better, but it ended up like usual."

The attitudes to the reform were age-specific. The participants in their 20s proved to be the least hopeful and most cynical. In general, this group was probably the most concerned about the current crisis in the country and feared more changes. They were also fairly critical regarding the prospects of reform, viewing corruption as the main barrier to its realization. Overall, the participants from this age group were passive in their engagement with anything political. They were especially concerned about the conflict in the east and the deterioration of relations with Russia, but they also did not seem to provide any ideas of how to address these problems. Participants from the two older age co-horts, 30-45 and 46-65, were more active in contemplating the possibilities of reform, but they still harbored substantial doubt about its realization. Overall, this group viewed corruption as being firmly embedded in state institutions, which was unlikely to change.

Similarly, there were some regional differences in the focus groups that are worth noting. In Kharkiv and Odessa, participants were more concerned about how recent events had severed ties with Russia, and in Lviv, people were predictably fully supportive of rapid integration into the EU. While the participants in Lviv were perhaps the most interested in civic activism, outside Kyiv, all focus groups were significantly concerned about problems of local governance. Interestingly, the participants in Kyiv were likely the least interested in the prospects for local government reform and were the least informed about the details of proposed decentralization.

If there were perceivable differences in the responses of participants from different age co-horts and regions, there was little evidence that responses could be differentiated by gender. To a certain degree, women participants were less pessimistic than men about the prospects of reform, but this did not hold true across all participants.

Perhaps the most important finding from the focus groups was the relative lack of information that participants had about decentralization reforms. Few participants were aware of the proposed status of the *hromada* as the primary unit of local self-governance, and even fewer were aware of its proposed functions and responsibilities under the proposed reforms. Participants also had some misperceptions about decentralization. Many viewed the process as merely a response to the conflict in the east and were not aware that the reforms are first and foremost intended to make governance more effective. Likewise, many participants were suspicious of the proposed institution of the "president's representative" on the local level, assuming that this was just another attempt to strengthen presidential power. Although this is a concern shared by many experts and will likely be addressed as the full structure of the reform is finalized, the participants generally saw no reason for any national-level control over local governance, suggesting a strong distrust of the national government.

These findings demonstrate the overwhelming need for the GOU to establish more widespread public discussion and education about proposed decentralization reforms. Although some efforts are being carried out to address this problem, the fact that almost nobody in seven focus groups around the country was knowledgeable about the proposed reform suggests that much more work needs to be done. Given the scope and scale of the proposed reforms, their success will be dependent largely on how they are perceived by the population. If the reforms are merely imposed on a citizenry that is ill informed about their purposes and their impact on them personally, there is a high likelihood of public resistance to them. In short, if these reforms are to be realized successfully, those implementing them must begin now building a constituency among the citizenry to support them.

Furthermore, citizens need to understand the risks of decentralization and the problems that may arise during its initial implementation. This is especially true with regards to the collection of taxes, the formation of local budgets, and public expenses. As local governments are authorized to collect taxes directly from citizens, for example, it is critical that citizens are aware of why this change is being implemented. Furthermore, decentralization will require a more active citizenry to hold local officials accountable and to participate in local decision-making. From the focus groups conducted, it was obvious that most citizens are not yet ready to take an active role in this process. Yet, given the ability to participate and information about how to do so, many likely would embrace the opportunity.

Finally, it is worth noting that local government reform was regarded by a substantial group of participants as untimely. Frequently, participants suggested that reforms should only be implemented once the economy is stabilized. As one participant from the 46-65 age co-hort in Kyiv stated, "today, this reform is impossible, you see. Impossible, because there are holes all around and they (the authorities) don't know what to do next." Others suggested that it was too late for Ukraine to undertake this reform and that it was not radical enough. As one participant from Kharkiv of the 30-45 age group noted, "decentralization would have been effective 5-6-10 years ago, now, everything has been so aggravated and dismal that something really radical is needed." However, these attitudes may just be reflections of doubt borne of past experiences about the potential for reform to be realized and make substantial changes in the way Ukraine is governed.

Overall, the focus groups suggested that decentralization has wide, but measured, support. At the same time, serious doubts exist as to the expediency of this reform, as well as the prospects of its successful implementation. These doubts are caused by several factors, including a lack of understanding of the proposed reform's details, a general distrust of government, past disappointments, and a fear of change. In this context, it will be critical to increase public outreach about these reforms before their implementation and establish modest but real expectations that they can improve life in the country.

IV. OTHER DONOR INVOLVEMENT IN DECENTRALIZATION

There are numerous donors involved in promoting decentralization in Ukraine, and many of them have been involved for numerous years, including in the later 1990s when the first law on local self-governance was adopted as well as during the Yushchenko presidency when the last serious effort to decentralize government was pursued. European donors have been especially involved in this effort, which is particularly appropriate given that the reform is meant to bring Ukraine closer to European integration by facilitating the country's compliance with the *European Charter on Local Self-Governance* and, hence, with the EU Association Agreement.[5] Additionally, the UNDP and the local manifestation of George Soros' Open Society Institute, the *Renaissance Foundation*, have played important roles in these efforts. As reforms continue in the post-EuroMaidan period, it is anticipated that most of these donors will continue to support the reforms with a variety of programming. Most existing donor projects related to local governance and decentralization fall into two categories: policy development support and local capacity building, mostly conducted on a pilot basis. At present, it appears that future programming will focus on these areas as well as on communications strategies for promoting and implementing reforms across the country. However, other donors are in a similar position to USAID at present and are assessing future needs as well as attempting to forecast how proposed reforms will actually be realized.

In the policy area, the Swiss SDC has been particularly involved and has supported the work of major local think-tank organizations, which have been the prime authors of reform legislation for the Ministry of Regional Development. Additionally the *Renaissance Foundation* is supporting this work through assistance to the local coalition of NGOs "reanimation reform package," which is helping to facilitate discussions between local experts, political leaders, and donors on the decentralization reform. Other players in this sphere include Canadian CIDA and GIZ to a lesser degree, but they have been less involved in recent reform efforts. In many ways, it makes sense to continue to allow those organizations already active in policy to take the lead into the future. The Swiss are well positioned as a neutral European country to provide this assistance without geopolitical implications while remaining focused on European standards, and the *Renaissance Foundation* is a completely locally

---

[5] For the text of the European Charter, see http://conventions.coe.int/Treaty/en/Treaties/Html/122.htm

run organization at this point. Furthermore, an over-abundance of players in the policy arena may only lead to a slowing down of reform. Other European donors will also be best placed to ensure that the policy framework for reform adheres to the EU Association Agreement recently signed by Ukraine. In this respect, the involvement of the Polish government is also critical. While Poland has not funded a large project on decentralization policy, it is providing advisors to the Ministry of Regional Development to assist with the process. This assistance is particularly important given that Ukraine intends to adopt a model based on that of Poland, and the decentralization reform in Poland has been quite successful. One would assume that such assistance would likely continue and maybe even increase once Ukraine begins the actual implementation of the reforms.

The other primary support provided to local governance has been through local-level development support and pilot projects, but this work to date has been quite scattered and has only focused on certain services and aspects of local governance. The Swiss have worked in five regions (Vinnytsia, Dnipropetrovsk, Ivano-Frankivsk, Poltava, and Sumy) where they have supported projects on communal services, particularly regarding water, and have promoted inter-municipal cooperation, and German GIZ has a similar project that has worked almost exclusively in Luhansk Oblast. The UNDP has worked on local development with local self-organized groups (also defined as *hromada*). This work has mostly involved community development efforts to address local needs (provision of school buses, repairing schools and health clinics, providing street lights, etc.), and it has reportedly worked with 1000 different communities around the country. However, this work is less focused on the administrative capacity of local governments to address local needs and is more concentrated on initiating local citizen involvement in local development. The German GIZ has begun a project on promoting the regional development policy process around the country. This work involves developing capacity among a group of regional development experts and establishing a network amongst them for the sharing of experiences. It will also fund regional development activities in regions and municipalities. The regional scope of this project at present remains unclear. Swedish SIDA is also beginning a new program in September that will focus on the monitoring of local service provision, mostly regarding administrative services such as licensing, and this will impact up to 12 small and medium municipalities.

Additionally, the EU more broadly has various funds to support local projects that are available to all European partner countries, including Ukraine. These include funds to promote cross-border communications between Eastern Europe and former Soviet partner countries, funds to help develop energy efficiency in small cities in European partner countries, and support for the development of neighborhood organizations available to municipalities throughout the European partnership countries.

Despite the abundance of donors involved in decentralization projects, there are many gaps in assistance, especially if reforms begin to be implemented rapidly in anticipation of the October 2015 local elections. Most donors with whom the assessment team spoke noted that the policy arena was already over-crowded, but there were endless needs not being met in terms of local development efforts, capacity-building, and citizen oversight.

Another area that seems conspicuously missing from present donor assistance involves the financial structures for decentralization. The most common problem with implementing decentralization reforms in the developing world involves the devolution of authorities to the local level without the allocation of sufficient resources for fulfilling these new responsibilities. A truly successful decentralization plan requires much more than altering the political structures of the country and empowering local authorities with increased responsibilities; it requires a complete restructuring of the public finance system of the country, including the ways that taxes are collected and by whom. It is noteworthy, for example, the most often stated constraint to effective local governance provided by interviewees was the lack of financial resources allocated to the local level (See Graph VIII). In regional cities, representatives of the Mayor's office also continually brought up the question of resources, noting that resources were more important that increased responsibilities since they already did not have the financial means to fulfill those responsibilities they already have.

Graph VIII: What are the biggest obstacles facing effective local governance?

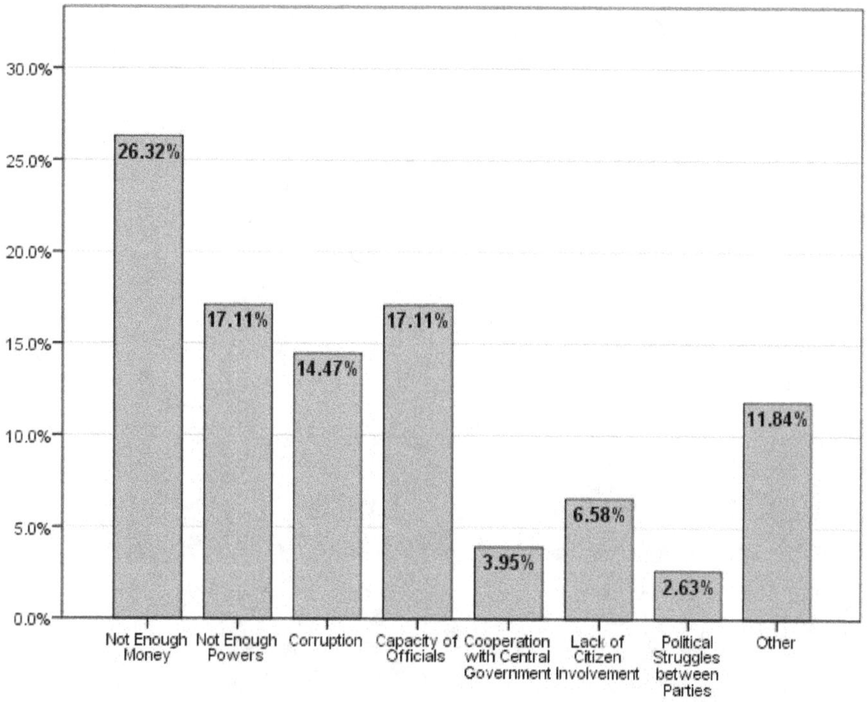

There are projects working on public finance with the Ministry of Finance, such as the one supported by USAID and a project supported by GIZ, but these have thus far operated within the assumptions of a centralized system for public finance. There remains a need for support to a reform of the financial system that allows for larger portions of state revenue to reach local municipalities and for a rational system of redistributing money from the national level to localities with less resources. This is a complex endeavor that requires the work of public financing experts familiar with various models of decentralization in the developing world and in Europe. Canadian CIDA had commissioned a white paper on fiscal decentralization for Ukraine in 2006 in support of anticipated decentralization reforms during Yushchenko's presidency, but it is unclear whether they plan to be involved in this area in the future.[6]

Additionally, there is a need for support to the Ministry of Regional Development regarding the promotion of a country-wide information and dialogue campaign to establish stronger public awareness of as well as buy-in and input for the proposed decentralization reforms. This is support that has been requested by the Ministry, and the EU is already considering support for such a program, but this is something that may need to be discussed among all donors so that efforts are not duplicated.

Finally, there does not appear to be substantial donor support for governmental accountability and citizen oversight on the local level. There are some initiatives of UNDP supporting e-governance efforts in various municipalities, but there is very little focus on the development of regional think-tanks, which can support local governments in strategic planning, or on citizen watchdog groups that

---

[6] "Fiscal Decentralization in Ukraine in the Context of Local Government Reform," Kyiv: CIDA, 2006 (http://icps.com.ua/pub/files/42/80/Fiscal_Decentralization_Eng.pdf)

can monitor local government revenue and expenditures as well as the activities of local council members as a check on corruption and abuses of power.